A Note to Parents

DK READERS is a compelling program for beginning readers, designed in conjunction with leading literacy experts, including Dr. Linda Gambrell, Professor of Education at Clemson University. Dr. Gambrell has served as President of the National Reading Conference and the College Reading Association, and has recently been elected to serve as President of the International Reading Association.

Beautiful illustrations and superb full-color photographs combine with engaging, easy-to-read stories to offer a fresh approach to each subject in the series. Each DK READER is guaranteed to capture a child's interest while developing his or her reading skills, general knowledge, and love of reading.

The five levels of DK READERS are aimed at different reading abilities, enabling you to choose the books that are exactly right for your child:

Pre-level 1: Learning to read
Level 1: Beginning to read
Level 2: Beginning to read alone
Level 3: Reading alone
Level 4: Proficient readers

The "normal" age at which a child begins to read can be anywhere from three to eight years old. Adult participation through the lower levels is very helpful for providing encouragement, discussing storylines, and sounding out unfamiliar words.

No matter which level you select, you can be sure that you are helping your child learn to read, then read to learn!

LONDON, NEW YORK, MUNICH,
MELBOURNE, and DELHI

Series Editor Deborah Lock
Managing Art Editor Rachael Foster
Designer Gemma Fletcher
U.S. Editor John Searcy
Production Georgina Hayworth
DTP Designer Emma Hansen
Jacket Designer Gemma Fletcher
Picture Researcher Rob Nunn

Reading Consultant
Linda Gambrell, Ph.D.

First American Edition, 2007
07 08 09 10 11 10 9 8 7 6 5 4 3 2 1
Published in the United States by DK Publishing
375 Hudson Street, New York, New York 10014

DK books are available at special discounts when purchased in bulk
for sales promotions, premiums, fund-raising, or educational use.
For details, contact:
DK Publishing Special Markets
375 Hudson Street
New York, New York 10014
SpecialSales@dk.com

Library of Congress Cataloging-in-Publication Data

DK readers Pre-level 1. My dress-up box / DK Publishing. -- 1st
American ed.
   p. cm. -- (DK readers)
Distinctive title: My dress-up box
Includes bibliographical references and index.
ISBN: 978-0-7566-2528-3 (pbk.)
ISBN: 978-0-7566-2529-0 (hardcover)
1. Children's costumes--Juvenile literature. 2. Children's clothing--
Juvenile literature. I. DK Publishing, Inc. II. Title: My dress-up box.
TT633.D54 2007
391'.3--dc22
                        2006023678

Color reproduction by Colourscan, Singapore
Printed and bound in China by L Rex Printing Co., Ltd.

The publisher would like to thank the following for their kind
permission to reproduce their photographs:
a=above; c=center; b=below; l=left; r=right; t=top
Alamy Images: Pegaz 17; Phototake Inc. 26; Mark Scott 18. Corbis:
Layne Kennedy 12-13 (b/g); William Whitehurst 30-31 (b/g). Getty
Images: Stone+/Siri Stafford 9. PunchStock: Digital Vision 15;
Photodisc Blue 4; Photodisc Green 19, 30l; Purestock 22; Stockbyte
11. Science Photo Library: John Sanford 29 (b/g).

All other images © Dorling Kindersley
For further information see: www.dkimages.com

Discover more at
www.dk.com

Contents

My
Dress-up Box

![DK] DK
DK Publishing

Here is my dress-up box.
What will I be?

I will be a princess.
Here is my crown.

crown

princess

ribbons

I will be a wizard.
Here is my cloak.

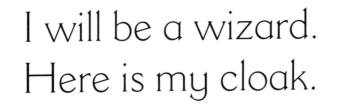

cloak

broom

wizard

hat

flag

pirate

I will be a pirate.
Here is my eye patch.

eye patch

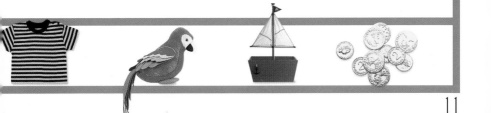

shell

mermaid

I will be a mermaid.
Here is my tail.

tail

I will be a cowboy.
Here is my hat.

hat

vest

cowboy

I will be a fairy.
Here are my wings.

wings

fairy

dress

superhero

I will be a superhero.
Here is my cape.

cape

shorts

tiara

tutu

ballerina

20

I will be a ballerina.
Here is my tutu.

overalls

worker

I will be a worker.
Here is my hard hat.

hard hat

I will be a firefighter.
Here is my helmet.

helmet

firefighter

hose

doctor

I will be a doctor.
Here is my patient.

patient

doctor

I will be an astronaut.
Here is my space suit.

space suit

astronaut

We are all dressed up.
Let's put on a show!

What will you be?

Glossary

 **Astronaut** a person who travels in space

 **Ballerina** a woman who dances ballet

 **Firefighter** a person who puts out fires

Mermaid a make-believe woman with a fish tail instead of legs

 **Princess** the daughter of a king and queen

Index